Please Still Love Me If I'm Happy

Dedication

To the still suffering addict
And to those
Who loved me while I suffered

<u>FRACTURED</u>

Lonely

The danger of connection
Is for a moment
You might feel okay

For a moment
You might believe you're worthy
Of love

And in a moment
All of that can be taken away

You can be alone again

It's easier to die
When nobody is watching

If I shoot myself
Amidst the silent falling trees
Will it make a sound

Empty I

It was a mistake
to let myself
Feel
Trust
Love

Who did I think I was

What made me believe
I'd survive this time

I'm not cut out
To live
And love
To let live
And let go

So I cut out
pieces of myself
And cry when I find myself
Empty

The Ocean

My mind is an ocean
Dark and unexplored
Thoughts crashing
Against my skull
Relentlessly

Peaceful at first glance
And terrifying
As you delve deeper

Don't try to get to know me
You'll drown

I'll swallow you whole
And they'll never find
Your body

Identity I

If nobody likes me
Am I nothing

What do I have to offer

Why can't I just like myself
Would that even be enough

I am lost
As I don't have the answers
And I don't even know
Where to begin
Finding them

Identity II

I don't know who I am
When I'm around you
And I don't know who I am
Without you

I found you at a time
Where I was lost
No direction
No wants
In need of help

Who would have known
When you thought you were building me up
You were actually building
A wall around me

Sabotage

If I meant to lose her
If I did it on purpose
Then why does it hurt

I suppose
The purpose
Was self-inflicted pain

I don't need a knife
To bleed

It hurts
Because I wanted it to

<u>Games I</u>

Don't make me small
Because I'll make myself known
By being a problem

Don't tell me I'm okay
Don't tell me it's nothing
Because then I'll show you something

And when the dust settles
And when I'm bandaged up
I'll realize that the only thing I've shown
Is that I'm capable of ruining my own life

I am left with guilt
And shame
And suffering

I intended to make a statement
To hurt those who have hurt me
Little did I know
I was the only one playing this game

<u>Choice I</u>

I was someone's first choice
Once

All she asked
Was for me to
Do
Say
Be
Everything she wanted

I was everything to her
At the small cost
Of entirely losing myself

If there ever was anything
To begin with

<u>Don't Speak</u>

They don't want to hear
Or listen
Unless it's a joke
Or a compliment
Or words of wisdom

People love you
When you're likable
Agreeable
Happy
Fun to be around

Nobody cares
How hard life is

They know
They suffer too

<u>Worthy I</u>

Why don't I think
They are lovely
If I don't think
Their body is lovely

Who taught me a woman
Is nothing
If nobody wants to fuck her

Play into the male gaze
Put yourself on display
Let us use you

That's all you're good for
Nobody wants you
If you don't put out

<u>Worthy II</u>
Would I be more lovable
If I was small like her

Do I need to be more funny
Or do I just never know the right words to say

Would people let me help them
If I proved myself

If I helped people
Then would I be worth something

I think these questions
That plague me
Say less about society
And more about me

I am the one
That thinks pretty girls
Are worth more

That lens that made me less than
Is the one I look through today

ACHING

<u>Memories</u>

What if every time I love
I give away a piece
And I'm slowly losing myself

What if in smashing myself
Into smaller and smaller bits
Thinking the more I leave behind
The more I'll be remembered

What if other people
Are collecting
Not giving away

Perhaps I'm supposed to be
Collecting and giving memories
As I have an eternal supply of those

Perhaps I was supposed to keep myself whole
This whole time

The Child I

The problem is
This is foreign to me

The problem is
I was born
And lived in
Chaos

The problem is
There is a small child
That begs for this consistent love
To stay

I am yelling at her
Telling her to stop crying
And to get over it

I am telling her
To push that love away

Does that make me cruel

I wish I could love her
The way she needs

Because I am the only one
Guaranteed not to leave

The Child II

I feel like a child
Who has lost her mother
And I'm in a room
With hundreds of women
That look just like her

Every time I run up to one
And they pick me up
And hold me
I cry
Because it doesn't feel
Like my mother

I am desperate
And I am lost

It is only when I run to
The one anomaly
A woman that has the same eyes
As me
That I am comforted

What happens if she leaves

What happens if she forgets
How to hold me

Identity III

I wonder if it's okay
That I'm doing okay

I wonder who I am
When I'm not screaming for help

I wonder if they are thinking of me
When I'm not begging for attention
Or if they've forgotten

I promise I want to love myself
Enough that I don't need to wonder

When the sun comes out
Do people really live
Without bracing themselves for clouds
And do they leave home without an umbrella

I miss the ignorance
The sad bliss of existential dread

The thing stealing my hope
Is my fear
Of hope

<u>Worthy III</u>
She sings like an angel
And he lights up the room

When they leave people talk about them
But not words of jealousy or hate
Words of admiration
He's my favourite
I love her

They are wanted
They claim to love me
But it's them
That everyone wants to be around

All I want is to be missed
When I leave a room

All I want is to be enough
All I want is to be paid attention to
All I want is to be everything to everyone

All I want is to be them
But I am me
And I am nothing

I hope I don't see the day
That they fall off the pedestal
I've put them on
It's a long way down

<u>Love I</u>

They'll love me until
I love myself
But how can I be loved
When my reflection
Makes me sick

It leads to pain
And suffering
And I'll fall apart
The moment they leave

I can't be loved
Without spending
Every waking moment
Chasing
Running
Until my lungs forget
How to breathe

I can't have faith
That a lack of affection
A lack of attention
Doesn't mean a lack of love

<u>Love II</u>
Tell me I'm good
Tell me you love me
Tell me I'm worth it

I won't believe you
But if you don't say it
I'll think you hate me

If one person
Says I'm good
I'll look at the 99 that didn't
And call myself
Unlovable

Love III

What it must be
To be loved
And not question

To be cared for
And not wonder
When it will stop

I am nothing
But a product of hate and lies

No wonder
I don't believe you
When you tell me
You'll stay

<u>Love IV</u>

Please tell me how to love myself
Tell me what it is I should love
Tell me you'll love me until I love myself
And then still love me when I do
And I know who I am

I see the greener grass
And I see everything in my path

There's a blade
And a line
And a bottle
And a joint
And every person I love on the sidelines
Cheering me on
But saying goodbye
For now

I am on the shore
Somehow drowning
Even though the tide is out
Because the moon is on my side

All I have to do is walk
But my legs won't work
If I feel unlovable

<u>Connection I</u>
How do I let people care
Without it hurting

How do I force myself to remember
To know
That people still love me
When I'm not sitting in front of them
When I am sad
When I have nothing to give
When I'm in pain

I get so scared
When people care
That I run in fear
And want to disappear

But I can't do this
Alone

Obsession

I am both empty
And consumed
Obsessed
And my head is also quiet

I find no comfort
In the space between

I find comfort in chaos

If I allow myself forgiveness
Give myself a break
And allow you to love me
Then I face the fact
That when you let go
And resume your day
I don't have the comfort
Of hating myself
Just the pain
Of you being gone

Each time we meet
It is like the first time
I have ever felt loved

Each time I see you walk away
It is like the first time
I have ever been left

Idolization

Oh how I wish
To live in the grey

For you to be neither
The best
Nor the worst

To see people
As simply that

People

I'm so sorry
To have put you on a pedestal
So high
That when you fell
It hurt us both

I'm so sorry
To have set you up
For failure

<u>Stay</u>

If I ask you to keep me warm
Will you hold me

And once I'm warm
Will you hold me still

I need you
In the dark
To guide me

But I still want you there
In the light

I promise it's worth it
To laugh with me
Just as much as it is
To cry with me

Promise me you'll stay
Even when I'm not
Broken and cold

So Kind

I wish I could call
To tell you I resent you
But I'm so kind

So kind of me to leave
Before you could leave me

So kind to carve
The messages I would send
Into my thigh
When you didn't pick up the phone

So kind to love you
More than I loved myself

I resent you
For letting me destroy myself
In your name

Choice II

Every time I choose you
I lose respect for me

I can't have both

I can't 100% choose myself
And keep putting you
At the top of the list

But I've been wrong before
I've made every bad choice
And it got me here

How am I to know
That this isn't the mistake
That ends me

Safety

I've never felt safe because of 4 walls
But I can tell you where I have

I felt safe
In the arms of the first girl
That promised not to leave
And actually stayed

But one day
She told me to die
And I wasn't safe
In my own head
Or home

I was safe in her arms
Until I felt alone in them

I felt safe
In the arms of the first girl
That promised me she understood me
And the thoughts in my head didn't scare her

But one day
She told me my love wasn't enough
And for a long time
I only felt safe
In the company
Of artificial happiness

I feel safe now
Amongst the ones I love

But I wonder what will happen
One day

Control I

There was a time
Where when people wanted to walk over me
I would lay down
And beg them to hold something heavy
So it hurt more

I have lied
Mostly about being okay
And I have begged
For things to go my way
But in truth
I didn't know how to ask

It is when I tell the truth
That I feel most vulnerable
When I give you the opportunity
To say no
To what I desperately need
I allow you to hurt me
And I don't want pain
This time

The crazy thing
About drawing lines in the sand
Is that the waves can effortlessly take them away
And the only hope is in
The tide being low
So I relinquish my control
To the moon

<u>Falling I</u>

As I hang off the cliff
You reach out to save me

At first I hold on tight
Scared and alone

You start to pull me up
And I start to let go

I want you to prove how much
You want to save me

Try harder
Pull harder

This ends in one of two ways

I let go
You fall with me

<u>Pain I</u>

How long
Can I keep hurting you

How long
Can I hurt myself
In your name

It's you or me
There is no winning
For us both

There is no compromise
This is do or die
For me

And I can't worry
About what it is
For you

Pain II

In that moment
When my heart hurt
And tears started to form
I realized two things

I truly
Honestly
And purely cared
For someone I neither knew
Long or well

And the tears
Were not only for her

The thing about this kind of pain
Is when you neglect it
It eats your soul

When a puppy barks
He doesn't stop
If you pretend you don't hear him
The only way out
Is through

Goodbyes I

I'm really scared to say goodbye
I've gotten used to this, you know
Who I can ask
When my brain lights on fire

How do I let everyone go
How do I accept that all of this care
Was temporary

How do I believe
That anyone will make me feel this safe

I know this is the nature of things
They start and they end
But I don't want endings
And I don't want beginnings
If anything
I want it to end now
So I can get started
On feeling the pain
And maybe let go

But I should have never grabbed on
In the first place

Goodbyes II

I thought I'd let go

Everyone saw through my lies
But I thought it to be true
I needed it to be

The only comfort
Is in black or white
Love or hate
Here or gone
Absolutely
And completely

I'm not okay
With the fact
That the moon only changes
A little bit each day
I want a new phase
Every time I sleep
Or maybe it could just stay
Full

Goodbyes III

Today I said goodbye
And hours later
I said hello again

It made my heart hurt
And I felt like I'd died
But it wasn't for a lack of affection

When I blink
I fear when my eyes open
They'll have disappeared

In all my efforts
To stop the snow from melting
When it rains
It doesn't help
When I watch

Unfortunately
Every time someone holds me
They let go
And I never know
When the next time will be

I never know the next time
It will rain
And I can't check the weather

<u>Letting Go I</u>
What happens if I let go

Is it you that has a chokehold on me
Or do I have my own hands
Wrapped around my neck

I am 5'6"
Standing in a 4' pool
Screaming that I'm drowning
Begging you to keep me afloat
And as you let go
You keep telling me
To just stand on my own two feet

How can I say you're letting go
When you've been walking beside me this whole time
Hands to yourself
But on the same journey

I am the only one that's holding on
And I don't know why

Why isn't it enough
To just have you by my side

If I do let go
If I stop begging you to stay
To love me
What will keep you here

How do I make sure you don't forget me
Without finding a way
To drown us both
In a 4' pool

<u>Silence I</u>

I promise I'm trying

Trying to love myself
More than I love others

Trying to save myself
Before I collapse
Into someone's arms

Trying to treat myself
Like I would treat a friend

It's so much easier to see
The good in her
Than the good in me
If it even exists

They tell me they see it
They tell me they love me

They don't know
That a star swallowed me whole
A long time ago
And sound doesn't travel
In space

Acceptance I

Somehow
It is not hard
To accept I will wake up
Not knowing the weather

Somehow
It is not hard
To accept she may never love me
As she once did

It pains me to accept
That people love me

That I may be happy

It disturbs me
To accept that this may be
Exactly where I am supposed to be

The fact I am pained and disturbed
Shows how little
I accept reality

Taste of Healing

My sadness feels like honey
In my chest
And I'm drowning
In sweetness

Every breath
Forms bubbles
That will never burst

I'm afraid to save myself

What if life tastes like
Lemons not lemonade

And how long
Can I burn my throat
Before I lose the ability to speak

Maybe honey and lemon juice
Is better than cigarettes and whiskey
But I'd really like to know
The peaceful emptiness
Of a happy exhale

CRAVINGS

<u>Satan, my saviour</u>
I think until my thoughts
Have thoughts

And I know all
Until I know nothing

And that's when I collapse
Disappearing into my shadow
With no light
To find my way back

As I'm falling a cold hand reaches
I'll catch you my love
Just sell me your soul
And I'll give you
Thin
White
Lines

Devil

The devil tells me
Everything I want to hear

He tells me life is about lust
Not love
And that all my problems
Can be taken away
If I just break my promises

He tells me there is no point
In being good
That good things come
To those that are bad
And it doesn't matter
Everything is temporary
So pay for 10 minutes of happiness

He tells me he loves me
And that he'll hold me
And that I don't need a soul

Give in to your impulse
Gamble your life
And the devil will catch you
When you inevitably fall

He will congratulate you
Welcome home

Powdered Happiness I

They told me once
Of magic

Inhale
And you will be free

Sell your soul
Sell your body
Sell your life
And you won't want it back

When that isn't enough
And you beg for sleep

When the birds start chirping
And the kids are on their way to school

When God offers you everything you've sold
At the small price
Of not believing in magic anymore

Tell him you'd rather live
In Hell

<u>Powdered Happiness II</u>
I've inhaled happiness before
Or maybe it wasn't happiness
But it took away problems
For a bit

I remember going to the ATM
Only $100
Right
But maybe I should take 2 or 3
So I don't have to pay the ATM fee tomorrow
Well maybe I should buy more
And save it for tomorrow

Maybe I should buy an 8 ball
And do it until my body begs for sleep
And have enough to start doing it again
When I wake up a few hours later

Maybe I should just do it forever
Maybe I should stay up for 52 hours
And tell everyone everything is fine
And do more and more and more
Until I want to die

Maybe right before I go to the ER
I should do a little more
So I don't have to go clean

Maybe when it tells me I don't have a problem
I should listen

Never had I loved anything
So much
That I'd rather die
Than never be with it again

Listen before I go
I never meant
For it to turn out
This way

I thought I had control
Power
Everything figured out

I know me best
Right

I know nothing

I have no will
When it comes to chemical happiness
I am nothing but a slave
To the darkness
And the light
At the bottom of a bottle

<u>Pain III</u>
When I was young
Everyone learned to colour
And I hated it
So I didn't

When I was 12
Strangers told me
I could learn to paint
If I kept it a secret

The only rule
Was to use red paint

I bought the supplies they told me about
And did my research

Only paint when you can't colour
They warned

Only paint
If you have to

When the pain was finally great enough
And I was truly ready
I sat on the bathroom floor
And painted myself red

I haven't got up since
And I forget
What colour
I used to be

Control II

I can't tell if I prefer when
My stomach
Or my brain
Is screaming

I beg her
To let me make it stop
But I beg myself
To be kind

Do I hate being full more
Or do I hate the look they give me
When I've done it
Again

Worthy IV

I failed
I didn't get bad enough

My scars are white
Not purple

I never scared people
With how little I ate
I never passed out in the grocery store

I never did enough
To OD
To need a drink in the morning
To shake

So when you say I'm doing well
I say I don't deserve this
I don't want this yet
Because you've seen Hell
And that's why I respect you

Attention

And what happens when I don't need to ask for help
At all hours of the day
Do people love me
Or do they love to help me
What do I have to offer when I'm not sad
Do I deserve your attention
When I just want to talk

These days I see a future
Where I hug myself when I'm sad and alone
And that's enough
But I don't want to be alone
All the time

I crave attention
I crave affection
I crave validation
Please oh please
Someone tell me I'm doing good
So I don't have to do bad again

Please still love me
If I'm happy

Trust I

I cannot trust
The voice that lives in my head
When I'm alone

I cannot trust
That you love me
Unless you tell me it's so

I can trust
A blade
And a line
And a drink

They have never failed me
But they will kill me

I cannot trust
Myself

Acceptance II

I wonder what would have happened
If I hadn't stolen booze
When I was 12
Or if I had gotten caught

What if I hadn't
Gone outside with him

What if he hadn't offered me
The vile of magical dust
That would ruin my life

I wonder
But I don't wish it to be different

I am in pain
And I am suffering
But I need to get to the other side
To reach the promised land

I thought I could inhale that place
But the only way
Is through

FAITHLESS PRAYERS

The Child III

I walked up to a little girl
And I told her
There is no God

Nothing is looking out for you
And nothing will save you
From this cruel world
There is nothing
For you to believe in

When she started to cry
I told her to stop
If there is no God
To wipe your tears
You might as well
Not shed them

Over the years
I saw the light fade
From her eyes
And the scars collect
On her wrist

She poisoned herself
Again and again
Hoping she would leave this world
And become nothing

Because she knew
The end was just that
The end

He saved her
Again and again

Today she prays
To never need saving
Again

But she knows
The world is a little less cruel
Than she had thought

<u>Faith I</u>

I put my faith
In wine stained lips
That promised
I would never be left

I put my faith
In a kid who drank too much
That promised
He wasn't like my dad

They failed me
So I put my faith
In myself

I woke up with scars
And an empty stomach

Faith II

It scares me to be seen

The tiny red mark on my wrist
Is unnoticeable
But they see through me when lie

My mind tells me I want to get worse
Do it again
Be more sneaky
Don't speak about your pain
Hide in plain sight
Hurt yourself and keep it to yourself
So nobody can be hurt by you

I couldn't hurt them even if I tried
And oh how I've tried

It strikes fear deep within me
To have faith
If I fail today
I'll wake up tomorrow
In good company

Forgive Me

Forgive me God
For I've done it again
And I ask that
You don't save me
This time

Forgive me
Because I'm tired
And this plan that you have
Is getting hard to be a part of

Forgive me
Because I don't want life
On life's terms

Forgive me
Because I want to choose
And I've been known
To make bad choices

Forgive me
Because I can't be
What you meant me to be

Uncertainty

I beg of you
Please tell me
Is God uncertain

Is He taking requests
And do I have any business
Telling Him
I am certain about what I want

Is certainty an illusion
For anyone
Other than God

Perhaps He is not playing chess
But rather
He is playing with the fabric of time
Like a cat with a ball of yarn

Entangled and linear
But complete

<u>The Moon</u>
I feel small sometimes
And then I remember

We put a man on the moon

Somehow we went
From picking poisonous berries
And hoping we don't die
To chicken nuggets
And AI

Somehow we went from slavery
To revolution
To obesity
To an epidemic
Of people dying on the street
With needles hanging out their arms

Somehow I went from crying
About scraped knees
To taking a blade to my wrist
To making lines with that same blade
To begging the man on the moon
To save me

I am somehow small
And tiny
And insignificant
In this universe
And simultaneously
Making people cry
With the words I write

Perhaps I am small to some
And everything to none
But enough

Control III

Today I got what I wanted
And I didn't need it

So was it wrong
For me to manipulate
To get it

Does God make sandcastles
Out of stardust
And then get told
He's interfering
With the trajectory of the big bang

Even if not
I am no God

Maybe tomorrow
I will let the universe
Decide my path

Guide my atoms
Dictate what collides

Free me from the prison
Of my decisions

Reality

If I was an optimist
I would say I'll get everything I want

If I was a pessimist
I would say it's going to be this bad
Forever

If I was a realist
I would say it doesn't matter
Because I will get what I need

I ask myself then
Why do people starve on the streets

I think the answer is faith
But it's bold of me to assume
That they didn't believe
And ask to be saved
On their death bed

All I ask
Is to know why bad things
Happen to good people
And as to why
They never get the opportunity
To heal

<u>Mistakes I</u>
Tell me Mr Moon
What do you see
While everyone sleeps

Do people dance in your light
Or do they cry and beg for answers

Have you ever given
What they asked for
Or only what they needed

I wonder if the only thing
You truly have control over
Is the tide

We're not so different
You and I

I too watched the world sleep

It was lonely
And unfortunately
You weren't good enough company

I wish you hadn't seen
What mistakes I made
In the dark

<u>Angels</u>
What mission has God given
The angels

I think I met one once
And she tried to save me
She cleaned up the blood
Bandaged me up
And told me she'd love me
Until I loved myself
She fell

I met another years later
And she tried to drag me down with her
She fell
As did I

I am finally surrounded by angels
All of them have seen Hell
And risen

I beg them to teach me
How to fly
They tell me they'll love me
Until I love myself
And my wings will grow
With time

This time I trust them
I wait patiently
I let them love me

I know
They will not let me fall

<u>Survival</u>

Maybe it's not about
The ones we lost

Maybe it's about
The ones who saved themselves

Maybe we thank God
For the ones that lived
To tell the tale
Instead of demanding answers
As to why others didn't

A boy I never knew
Wrote his last words
Not all of us are meant to survive

If that's true
Good thing He decided
We're meant to

Part Of

What it must be
To be a rock in the river

Slowly eroding away
With every second of running water
And yet
Becoming more a part of the river
Every moment

Something more

There is nothing and everything
Passing by
Never staying for long
And yet
Always making an impact

Is it so wrong
To watch the pretty things
Float by
As we fade away

Acceptance III

How am I to accept this pain

If I put my faith in God
I must ask why this is his plan for me

I know I was meant to die
A few times
And I am grateful
To have been spared

But it must be
Some kind of cruel joke
To keep me alive
Just to experience more pain
Than death itself

I would like to believe
That I am receiving everything I need
And accept
That this is exactly how things are meant to be

I am no God
And I wish to stop impersonating him

So I beg
Please give me
What you think I need

And I beg
Take this obsession
Away from me

<u>Faith III</u>

For all the times
I risked my life
I thank you for saving me

For all the times
I chose darkness
I thank you for making the sun rise
Again

All I know
Is that I know nothing
And that's okay

When all else fails
And when all is going well
I will have faith
In the inevitable

Letting Go II

And on this day
I let her go

I did not say goodbye
And I didn't stop loving her

My memories were not stolen
And I did not lose her

Somehow I let her go
And she didn't disappear

I let her walk away
And when the sun rose
We went for coffee

I don't let her go
For her to be free of me

Rather
I let our paths diverge
And have faith
That if they cross again
We will walk together
As old friends

I let her go
So I may be free
Of playing God

Perhaps I will make friends
With the trees

<u>Choice III</u>
Perhaps loving yourself
Is less of a journey
And more of a decision

I begged God to tell me
How I could gain the strength
To love myself

He showed me
The birds don't get self conscious
When they sing their songs

And the trees aren't embarrassed
When one of their branches breaks

The decision is not in the words
I love myself
But rather
It is found in the moment
I accept myself
As being exactly
How I am supposed to be

God told me
He doesn't make mistakes

<u>Almost Okay I</u>
It's more comfortable to say
I hate myself
Than to admit
Things might be kind of okay

I might be a little happy
I might be enjoying this
I might be getting somewhere

But even if I admit that
My immediate thought is
When will I fuck it up

RESURRECTION

Enough

I fear the darkness
The unknown
And I am without a flashlight

I scream into the void
And I cry
Running further and further away
From what I know

I am lost

A girl I barely know
Runs after me
And lights a match

This is all I have

And it's enough
Because I'm not alone

Serenity

There is no serenity
In highs and lows

Serenity is in the grey
A few feet under
Not drowning on the ocean floor

Serenity is in the space between words
Not in the calm
Before the storm
But in the light drizzle
Before it pours

Serenity is where you least expect it

<u>Light</u>
On the darkest night
I learned to shine
With my own light

Not entirely in a day
But a spark
Entered my heart
And it was enough
To light a fire

Every day
I make an offering

I will give myself
All my power
Over to the elements
To become brighter

I allow myself
To be guided by the universe
In hopes that one day
I will shine like the stars

<u>The Forest I</u>

I was lost
When I entered the forest
And I let delusion guide me

It's a well worn path
And I was walking it for years

Eventually my legs started to give out
And somehow with nothing to my name
My bags were breaking my back

On the darkest of nights
When the moon had been stolen from the sky
I heard a voice in the distance
"Follow the stars"

And I did

A girl sat in a tree
No fear of falling
And full of laughter

She claimed she had walked the same path as me
And now she was free
And she saw herself in me

She promised the true path
The one less travelled
Was clear with a good vantage point

She didn't save me
But she gave me a map
And I am eternally grateful
To finally have freedom on the horizon

The Forest II

Trees do not cry
When they lose their leaves
And everyone exclaims
How pretty

We admire the scarcity
Of a beautiful ending
And accept
That everything
Is temporary

Winter will come
And colours will fade
But impending doom
Doesn't stop the kids
From diving into an orange and red sea

The eternal Forest
Allows us to fall
And fall again
So we may see
True beauty

Resistance

So don't take it as being hard on you
And so I took it as being hard on me
And that was the perfect example
Of the problem

My friends come to my house
And write in bright red ink
How much they love me
On the windows
And I shut the blinds
So I can beg them to come inside

Tell me I'm good
So I can ask how good

The ones who claimed to love me before
Only kissed me
If I was bleeding
Because they needed to make it better

Today I took a hot shower
Instead of cold
Because that felt more like a hug
And when I looked myself in the mirror
I told the person looking back at me
That they're not the problem
But they can be
And then I opened the blinds

Powerlessness

It is not weak
To be powerless

Rather
Accepting our lack of power
Makes us strong

It is not weak
To face reality

Whether it is love
Or drugs
I am only free
When I give up
Thinking the power
Lives within me

It is not weak
To accept there are many things
Greater than me

Letting Go III

The feeling is so foreign
So foreign I cannot even name it

Do I feel safe
Am I happy
Is this what trusting people is like
Have I finally let people care

Perhaps yes to all

Today I let go
Of my suffering
And a weight has been shifted
Not lifted
But put on the back burner

Today I felt loved
Without needing to give
To earn it

I know this will not last forever
There will be bad days again
But for once
I believe I'll survive
And I will not bring the bad
Upon myself
Intentionally

Freedom

I thought I inhaled freedom

I thought my pain
Kept me in a cage
And every time
I did a line
The door unlocked

She couldn't hurt me anymore
She couldn't control me anymore
Nobody could
Or so I thought

Little did I know
I was a slave
Every night and
Every day
I wasted away
Begging for another trip
To the promised land

It is today
When I have given up
Everything I knew
Every comfort I had
That I am free

It is today
That I sit down with my pain
And have a coffee

<u>Mistakes II</u>
I went from
thin white lines
to thin red lines

I try to argue
with myself
And with God
that it is the lesser
of two evils

He spoke to me
through my tears

You don't deserve either

So I put down the blade
And picked up the phone
And picked up the pen

I made a mistake
I'm not a mistake

Mistakes III

I gave in to my impulse
And I gave up

This time I didn't expect someone
To save me

This time my day
Isn't ruined

It was a good day
And a bad moment

I have not failed
I took a step back

The good thing
Is I've been walking forward
For a while now
And the view looks better
And I can see the bigger picture

From back here

Games II

When I speak
How do I ensure
You hear me

Probably by listening

Sometimes I think
If I speak in pretty words
If my thoughts sound like songs
You'll sing along

I must stop playing this game

It is nothing less
Than a privilege
To be let in
To the confines of your mind

The most precious gift
I can give in return
Is my silence
Until I am asked to speak

Connection II

The rain falls
And she hugs me
And I can finally breathe

I cry under the covers
And she sits down in front of me
And takes breaths for me

The panic sets in
And I don't know
How I'll ever get out of this
And she tells me
It's okay
Just live through today

The beauty is in the fact
That she is not just one person
And there will always be another

The beauty is in the fact
That when she is no longer in front of me
A spot will have opened
And I will trust again

Connection III

Whether it is a day
A month
A year
Or forever
That they leave for
I will be okay

I will wake up
And I will fall asleep again

Coffee will still taste good
And laughter will still fill me with joy

Maybe I will miss them
Perhaps even forever
And I will still feel loved

When I cry
There will still be a shoulder
Perhaps just not a familiar one

I will always hope they come back
And if they don't
I will be okay

Choice IV

The only choice
I absolutely need to make
Is if I wish to live
Another day

Say yes
And everything else
Falls into place

Micro decisions are simply
Asking what direction
I will step in

This is not an illusion

The path to life
And the path to death
Are both clear

Today I choose life
And everything else
Can be dealt with
Tomorrow

Choice V

I could hurt you
Or myself
But I won't

We would survive
And the sun would still rise
But for how long

I have made every wrong decision
And to my surprise
I still get the opportunity
To decide to make the right one

The beauty of falling down
Is that all you must do
Is decide to get up

I get to decide
To see the sun rise
Again

Falling II

If you fall
It's of no use
For me to jump after you
Without a parachute

It's also of no use
To jump off a cliff
In hopes
That someone will save me

Maybe I should just go
Buy a parachute
For when I inevitably fall
And save myself

Trust II

I trust in suffering
I trust that in my darkest moment
I will feel around
And find a flashlight

I trust that on the day
I wish for death
I will find a reason to laugh

I trust that I will not wake up
With my goals
A centimeter away from me
And that the beauty will be
In the process

I trust that everything I have felt
Is both unique
And able to be felt again

I may be moving forward
But that doesn't mean
I lose what is behind me

The Cure

If I could take a pill
To cure me
I don't think I would

Not because I don't wish
To be spared of my suffering
But because I need the gifts
Born from it

I thank the devil
For letting me live in Hell
Not because I enjoyed it
But because things don't burn me
So easily now

I get to stand in front
Of those with paper skin
And say I understand

Reality

Unfortunately
Everyone dies
And almost everyone relapses
And a lot of people that relapse die
At the hands of their addiction

Unfortunately
I can't save anyone

Unfortunately
I will never know
The outcome
Of doing yesterday
Differently

Fortunately
Nobody died today

Fortunately
I get to try and be better
Tomorrow

Truth

Unfortunately
Starving myself
Still brings me joy
Even when I don't tell a soul

Unfortunately
I no longer feel that joy
When I admit to my wrongdoings

Fortunately
That makes others proud

Fortunately
That means I have a chance
Of doing the right thing
Tomorrow

<u>My New Life</u>
When I am in pain
I get to cry
And remember why
Afterwards

On my worst days
I know it will get better
And on my best days
I know it will get better

I have died
To come back
To a new life

It is full of laughter
And love
And pain
That I would not trade
For the life
That got away

I get to live today

Acceptance IV

And in desperation
I wronged myself
And others

In desperation
I forgive myself
For my wrongs

When I do bad
I am not bad

My actions
Define me
And also don't

One day
I will align with my values

Every day
I will try to do better than yesterday

I will wake up
And embrace
The day that I am meant to have

Grace

Perhaps I don't need to be
Perfect

I think everyone hurts
The ones they love

Maybe the world doesn't implode
Every time I make a mistake

Unfortunately you cannot give me the grace
I so desperately need

Yes, you have given me grace
But I can still hate myself
When you love me
Through my wrongdoings

Your forgiveness is not enough
But inside it feels as if
You are the only one that can heal this wound

I accept this responsibility

I will apologize
And I will forgive myself
And if you leave
I will say it wasn't meant to be

I am not that powerful
I may only walk
The path I am presented with

I am doing the best I can
And that needs to be enough

Self Esteem

Why does my self esteem
Rely so heavily
On what others think of me

Why do I hate myself
Every time you leave
Why can't I just miss you
Purely
And simply
Miss you

Why do I make it about me
And my identity

Who is the self
In self esteem

I don't know if it is my
Mind
Body
Or soul

All I know
Is it's not you

So I stare down the one in the mirror
And ask
Who do you want to be

The figure in the reflection tells me
Everything we already are
We are everything we are meant to be
It is enough

I walk away
Knowing what I think of me

Worthy V

What if for one second
Perhaps a mere minute
I let myself believe I'm
Enough

Would there be an avalanche
In my head
Or would I move mountains

Would I look in the mirror
And not flinch at my own reflection
Perhaps I would notice
Just how often my eyes change colour

Would I live just as freely
After things start to get good

Maybe my worth
Is not in my sadness
Perhaps I can bring light
Without consuming all the darkness

Maybe I could try to choose
Every second
To live for another
Not just survive

Split

He is everything I fear

He is the darkness in the back of my head

He is what I want to do but don't let myself

He feeds off attention

He lives for validation

He is defiant

He pushes everyone away

He is hurt

He hates himself

He lives in a constant state of pain

He waits for someone to save him

He is me

I no longer want to be him

Love V

I said I love you
For the first time today
And he said
Take care

Suddenly I was 12 years old
With a knife in my hand
Begging to know why I was so unlovable

Suddenly I was 15 in the Arizona heat
Drunk and crying
Begging to know why she left me
Again

Suddenly I was 25 on her bathroom floor
Sticking my fingers down my throat
Begging to know why I wasn't good enough
To touch

I'm not in need of answers

I have to let go

Identity IV

I can't save you
I can't change you

I would love to
But I tried
And I lost myself

How can I be me
When I am you

How can I live
When I am living for you
By your rules

I want to live for myself
My way

Empty II

Please someone tell me
Why it hurts so much
To love people
Tell me how
I'm supposed to accept that goodbye
Is usually see you later
And that that's okay
Tell me how
I'm supposed to fill this hole in my chest
Without just building my pieces
Around someone I love

I am fractured
My body gapes
With the shadow of the last girl I loved
I tried to pour booze into it
And cut it to pieces
With thin white lines
But to no avail

All my efforts make it
So that now
Not even she will fill the hole

I am filling myself with poetry
And books
And yet I still feel empty

I need to fill myself with love
But not for another
Not for someone that can leave

This hole is shaped
Like me

<u>Gratitude I</u>
I am grateful

For my pain
And for the moon

For everyone that hurt me
And for those that helped me

For the strength I was given
When my dad didn't love me
And the peace that came
When he did

For the times I almost died
And to be alive

Gratitude II

I thank the universe

For the holes in the clouds
That let me see the moon

For the ones who make me laugh
Especially when I want to cry

For the ones who are kind
When I am not

For the ones that trust me
When I might not deserve it

For the poems and songs
That have kept me alive

For saving me and sparing my life
When I tempted fate

I thank the universe
For love
And laughter
And my life

Hope I

I want it so bad

I want to love
I want to be loved
I want to cry
And I want a shoulder to cry on

I want the future I gave up on
I want what I wanted when I was honest
I want what I think I can't have
But maybe I can

Maybe I'm not in control of getting what I want
But I can try things
And stay alive
And let life take me
Where I'm supposed to go

I'll never arrive
But I'm learning to love driving
And not necessarily having directions

Hope II

I think there's hope for me yet
I think there's hope
In the fact that I've changed
In the fact that I'm loved
And in believing in myself

I was convinced that life was not for me
And now I'm convinced there is a path for me
To follow

This path goes through the depths of hell
And through clouds
And sunsets
And sunrises
It winds
And cracks
And takes me everywhere I've never been

It takes me
Where I am meant to be

Although I know nobody will walk
An entire lifetime with me
I hope the ones with me now
Stay a while

Hope is on the horizon

Hope III

There's hope in the fact
That when clouds die
They are reborn
And when people tell me they love me
They mean it
And when I look in the mirror
I don't die inside anymore

When I make jokes
Sometimes people laugh
And when I cry
People hold me
And eventually I'm okay

When I sit in my room
I sometimes don't feel alone
And when I can't sleep
The stars keep me company

There's hope in the fact
That today I don't want to die
You could even go as far to say I want to live

And the next time I want to die
There will be hope in the fact
That I know I'll survive

Because I always have
And I always will
Until I no longer want to

Positivity

I flip a coin
Yell tails
And it lands on heads

Do I cry
Or do I flip it over

Do I sit in darkness
Or do I search for the moon
To guide me
With light

Sometimes
The sun will shine upon me
And others
I will have to chop down a tree
Just to survive
Just to have heat

We cannot just let it be
We must look for positivity

<u>Humility</u>
All I know is that
I do not know

So I listen

I listen to the trees
When they speak
Through the rustling
Of leaves

I listen to those
Who have survived
Longer than me

No
They have lived
Longer than me
Perhaps not in age
But in liberty

Almost Okay II

Maybe I'll be okay

Maybe if I look at the moon
That's bright in the middle of the day
Or look at the clouds
That make the sky look like an ocean
Or feel the jagged edges of a rock
I can live to the next second

Maybe if I read a book
Or write a poem
Or accept that things that hurt
And reasons they are valid
Can exist at the same time
I can go without destroying myself

Maybe if I let myself be okay
And let myself hurt
When things hurt me
I can move on

<u>Almost Okay III</u>

There's a possibility that one day
Everyone I love will be a distant memory
And I will be okay

There's a possibility that one day
The number I'm so very proud of
Will go to zero
And I will be okay

One day I will let her fall
Off the pedestal I have put her on
And there's a possibility
I will feel alone
And lonely
And lost
And I will be okay

When the name of someone I know
Is plastered upon the wall
With the other fallen soldiers
I will be okay

When I put my faith in someone
And it is misplaced
I will be okay

When I am so hurt
Or scared
Or bored
That I feel like I'm dying
I will be okay

When I am not okay
I will be okay

Almost Okay IV

On my knees
I beg for someone
To ask me what's wrong

And when they do
I say nothing
Because I have no other way
To ask for love

I look for things to hurt me
So I can ask you
For a band-aid

It doesn't matter
If I metaphorically
Or physically
Slash my wrist
Someone always comes to my rescue

I am tired of bleeding out
And I think the people that love me
Are running out of bandages

Maybe it's okay to ask
For coffee instead
And talk about everything
That kept us alive

Maybe I don't need to die
To be remembered

Maybe nothing's wrong
And that's okay

Almost Okay V

Maybe it's okay that I've died a couple times
Maybe I was meant to

Perhaps I lost myself
Simply so I could find myself again

Build myself up
Not from broken pieces
But from things I found along the way
When I kept moving forwards

Maybe I'm not who I was
And maybe I'll never be that again
But that doesn't mean I'm not me

I am not nothing
I am not empty
I am a constant project
Being built and destroyed
Simultaneously always complete
And never done

<u>Almost Okay VI</u>
A cloud died
In front of my eyes today
And I tried to be okay with it

A conversation had to end today
And I tried to be okay with it

I realized my heart hurts today
And I tried to be okay with it

I'm not okay today
And I'm trying to be okay with it

The cloud will form again
And I will speak to her again
And one day I'll be happy again
And maybe tomorrow I'll be okay again

But for now
I'm okay with how today is

Almost Okay VII

Perhaps I no longer enjoy the chaos

Maybe
Just maybe
I want to experience the joy
Of someone saying hi
Instead of what's wrong

I am ready to be loved
Freely
And without begging

I am also done
Begging myself to be kind

I want to be okay

I want fuzzy blankets
And good music
And snacks
And warm drinks
And the ability to enjoy it all
Alone

I want to be okay

I will be okay

<u>Innocence</u>

I wish I could go back

To when I wore swimsuits
And didn't think people
Would talk about my body

To when drinking and driving
Was confusing
Because I thought it was about soda

I wish I could skip to the part
Where it gets good

The point in the plot
That everyone has been waiting
For the hero to reach

If only
That destination existed

Honestly
I'm alright with never arriving
Just driving

It's about the journey

The Garden

When I crack open my chest
And look at the garden within
I'm scared to know what I'll find

Will it be a barren wasteland
My lungs deflated
And the skeletons of my past
Poking out of the soil

Will there be flowers
Or thorns
In the space between my ribs

I have to plant seeds

I want sunflowers
And daisies
And life
To radiate from within me

I want to be beautiful
Not broken
Or perhaps
Beautifully broken

<u>The Beach I</u>
Who let you
Paint the sky

Who let you
Make a mosaic
Of the mountains
Across the sea

Days are long
So I bury myself in the sand
And beg the tide not to take me

I must see you
Before you leave

You bring me peace

The Beach II

In that moment
I vowed to mend my heart
With the broken sea shells I found

Because tiny fragments
Could make me whole again

Tranquility

Before
Tranquility was found
In chaos

Waves crashing against jagged rocks
And tempting fate
Seeing if I live or die

Knowing I shook hands
With death
And lived to tell the tale
Brought me peace

I have learned now
Of the tranquility found
In soft blankets
And gentle hugs
Given without expectations

I have found tranquility
In safety

<u>Silence II</u>
I wish I knew
The silence

But I am faced
With the chatter
Of my mind
And the echos
Of goodbyes

If I close my eyes
And the blanket hugs me
Just right
I hear her
Tell me she's in love with me
For the first time

The world is full of sirens
And crying babies
And music for people to dance to
But we would only find silence
If no one was around to hear

Maybe I'm okay
With the volume of my mind

It means I'm alive

<u>Ink</u>
Spilt ink
Spills my thoughts
And I let go

I don't love it
But I need it

When you hurt me
I write

When I'm sad
I write

When I'm in love
I write

When everything in the world is wrong
I write it

My pen releases me
From the prison that is my mind
And what was once solved by lines on a mirror
Is solved by sharing lines on paper

If I write
And nobody listens to me read
It doesn't make a sound
But I am still free

To Those Who Keep Showing Up

I forget they are human too

It is a logical fallacy
To provide care
And be expected
To not care
Beyond the confines of a building

On behalf of those
Still suffering
I apologize for the anticipation

On behalf of those
Whose brain tells them
To act on selfish impulse
I vow to try
To let you care
To remember I matter

To care about myself

To live
Not just survive

Dreams

When I was young
I dreamed
Of dinosaurs
And drowning

When I was a little older
I decided
I wanted to learn
To control my dreams

What a lucid thought

It was not until
I forgot how to dream
That I realized
The dreams you control
Are those you have
When you're awake

Dear my future self
If you're reading this
We lived

Through the pain
And suffering
And laughter
And heartbreak

If you're reading this
It wasn't all for nothing

The beauty is in the fact
That you could read this
Tomorrow
Or 5 years from today
And simultaneously
Everything and nothing
Will have changed

We lived to see another day

Love VI

My name means loved one
But I feel so unlovable
Not because I am
But because it's scary to be anything else

What happens if I let you love me
Let you care for me
Let you help me

If I don't get better
Will you leave

If I ask 100 times
And I still need to ask 101st
Will you still give it to me

Do I have anything to offer

These are the questions that play
Inside my head
On a never ending loop

I'm starting to get answers
And they are full of light
And hope

For once
I might let you stay
I might not push you away
I might deserve you
And maybe you deserve me too

Love VII

Maybe today people love me
And I can accept that love

Maybe they really truly love me
And they might stay

Maybe not everyone
walks away

Even if they do
They come back
When and if they are meant to

I want to let people in
Let them do
What I do for others

Maybe I'm good enough
Maybe
Just maybe
I deserve love
And happiness
And acceptance

Finally Okay

The kid that saw no future
Would be so proud

I wish I could convey
How it feels
To get through hard things
And come out the other side
In one piece

I may be broken
And glued together
But my jagged edges
Are slowly getting less sharp

I don't panic
At every goodbye
Anymore

Today
I am okay

The End

So I was laid to rest
And as people gathered around
They knew it wasn't
Because I was tired

They cried
Not because of tragedy
But because they would miss me
Happily

The room was full
Of people I helped
And people I loved
And people that loved me

The room was full
Of love
Not pain

80 years
On the tombstone
And the words
She lived a good life

Please Still Love Me If I'm Happy
Copyright © 2025 by Priya Wadhwa
All rights reserved. No part of this book may be reproduced, stored in a retrieval system, or transmitted in any form or by any means — electronic, mechanical, photocopying, recording, or otherwise — without the prior written permission of the author, except in the case of brief quotations used in reviews, articles, or academic analysis.

ISBN: 9798296610874

First Edition

Cover design by Gabrielle Madden

Printed by Amazon Kindle Direct Publishing

Printed in Dunstable, United Kingdom